How Does the Holy Spirit Work in a Christian?

By Kyle Pope

How Does the Holy Spirit Work in a Christian?

By Kyle Pope

© **Truth Publications, Inc. 2019. Second Printing.** All rights reserved. No part of this book may be reproduced in any form without written permission from the publisher. Printed in the United States of America.

ISBN:1-58427-253-8
ISBN: 978-158427-253-3

First Printing: 2009

Truth Publications, Inc.
CEI Bookstore
220 S. Marion St., Athens, AL 35611
855-492-6657
sales@truthpublications.com
www.truthbooks.com

Contents

Preface 5

The Triune Nature of God 7

The Holy Spirit's Role in Inspiration 10

The Holy Spirit's Work in the Individual Christian 16

When the Holy Spirit Speaks: Strong Feeling or Words? 41

Can It Be Proven from Scripture that Miraculous Spiritual Gifts Have Ceased? 45

Scripture Index 61

Preface

The material presented in this book was originally written in connection with some online discussions I had with denominationalists over a period of weeks in the spring of 2008. Although the topic did not begin with a discussion of the work of the Holy Spirit, it became evident that the views that many in the religious world hold regarding the work of the Holy Spirit color all aspects of their understanding of Biblical topics. These denominational concepts far too often find their way into the church in the language we use, and unscriptural notions we gradually adopt. This study is an attempt to carefully "weed out" concepts that are rooted in the theories and theologies of men in order to isolate the pure revelation of God on this most important question. My prayer is that the reader will test all things presented in the pages that follow by the infallible standard of God's word, accepting only what is found to be true to the Holy Spirit revealed oracles of God.

Kyle Pope

Chapter One

The Triune Nature of God

The question posed in the title of this study is an important matter of consideration for all who would seek to understand the role of the Holy Spirit in the life of a Christian. To address this question we must first consider who the Holy Spirit is. The Bible teaches that the God who made all things is one God (1 Corinthians 8:6), composed of three persons: God the Father, God the Son, and God the Holy Spirit (Matthew 28:19). This is a difficult concept for our mortal, finite minds to grasp—but it is the teaching of Scripture. Each person of the Godhead, has His own distinct will. Jesus in the garden, prayed to the Father, **"not My will, but Yours be done"** (Luke 22:42, NKJV). He promised His disciples that when the Holy Spirit came upon them, **"He, will not speak on His own authority, but whatever He hears He will speak"** (John 16:13). So, the Holy Spirit is not simply a different manifestation of the Father. Rather, He is a distinct person of the Godhead. The Father is not the Son, the Son is not the Father, the Holy Spirit is neither the Father nor the Son, yet they are not *three gods*—they are all *one God*.

The Triune Nature of God

With regard to the "personhood" (so to speak) of the Holy Spirit, we must concede that it is a difficult concept for man to grasp how there can be one God (1 Corinthians 8:6) composed of three persons. However, the evidence of Scripture demands that we come to this conclusion. Far too many notions in the religious world confuse this truth. Many diminish the Holy Spirit to simply an extension of the Father's presence. This fails to acknowledge the Spirit as a full and complete member of the Godhead.

Within this Godhead there is distinction, but also unity. Scripture on occasion speaks of Father, Son, and Holy Spirit doing the same thing. A case in point is the indwelling. The body of the Christian is said to be the **"temple of the Holy Spirit"** (1 Corinthians 6:19), yet, the Christian is also told, **"God has sent forth the Spirit of His Son into your hearts"** (Galatians 4:6). To the apostles, it was said of their indwelling, **"it is not you who speak, but the Spirit of your Father who speaks in you"** (Matthew 10:20). This demonstrates clearly that all three persons are divine—all are one God.

Scripture elsewhere makes the distinction of personhood clear in regard to both will and locality. In the texts cited above—first, in Jesus' statement in the garden, we see the Son say to the Father, **"not My will, but Yours be done"** (Luke 22:42). If Jesus had a *will* that was distinct from the Father's, then He possessed distinct personhood. Second, it is said of the Holy Spirit that, **"He, will not speak on His own authority, but whatever He hears He will speak"** (John 16:13). If the Spirit were merely an extension of the Father then His words would be under *His own authority*. This distinction is shown in regard to lo-

The Triune Nature of God

cality in the baptism of Jesus. God the Son (on earth) was baptized. God the Father (in heaven) spoke. God the Holy Spirit descended as a dove (Luke 3:21-22). This may be difficult to conceptualize, but we must accept Scripture for what it says and be content with what Deity has chosen to reveal about itself (cf. Deuteronomy 29:29).

There is a very ancient graphic that attempts to illustrate what Scripture teaches on this matter. It was originally written in Latin, but it is translated it into English on the right. It shows that while all three person are all one God, each bears its own distinction from the other.

The symbol on the previous page, adopted as the logo for New King James Version, published by Thomas Nelson Publishers, is another ancient graphic known as the *triquerta*. It illustrates in the same way that the God of the Bible is one God composed of three persons. To understand the manner in which the Holy Spirit works in a believer, any concepts framed to explain this must harmonize with this fundamental truth of Scripture. There is one God, of three distinct persons. The Father is not the Son. The Son is not the Holy Spirit. The Holy Spirit is neither the Father nor the Son. Yet, they are all one God.

Chapter Two

The Holy Spirit's Role in Inspiration

The Bible teaches that the Holy Spirit has played an active role in the revelation of Scripture throughout the history of God's dealings with mankind. Peter wrote:

> …**No prophecy of Scripture is of any private interpretation** [most footnotes say *or origin*] **for prophecy never came by the will of man, but holy men of God spoke as they were moved by the Holy Spirit.** (2 Peter 1:20-21)

This fact is reflected in Paul's words to Timothy that, "**all Scripture is given by inspiration of God**" (2 Timothy 3:16). In the original Greek the phrase "given by inspiration of God" is one word—*theo-pneustos* meaning literally "God-breathed." That means that while the books of Matthew, John, or First Peter were written by those apostles who bear their name, these men were directed to write the things they wrote by the Holy Spirit. Jesus said the same of the psalmist, King David, referring to a text which he had written, declaring "**David in the Spirit**" said, such and such (Matthew 22:43).

The Holy Spirit's Role in Inspiration

The Bible reveals a very special role that the Holy Spirit would have in connection with the gospel of Jesus Christ. This role was prophetically foreshadowed even before Jesus came to earth. Joel proclaimed:

> **And it shall come to pass afterward that I will pour out My Spirit on all flesh, your sons and your daughters shall prophesy, your old men shall dream dreams, your young men shall see visions. And also on My menservants and on My maidservants I will pour out My Spirit in those days.** (Joel 2:28-29).

On the day of Pentecost after Jesus' ascension when the Holy Spirit came upon the twelve apostles and they spoke in tongues, Peter referred to Joel's words declaring that what was happening on that day was, **"what was spoken by the prophet Joel"** (Acts 2:16) going on to quote from the prophet. This was a marvelous thing. The Old Testament had recorded many times in which there had been a prophet or a small group of prophets, but never before had there been such a widespread outpouring of the Spirit. The only other time had been when the Spirit "rested upon" the seventy elders in the wilderness through whom God instructed the Israelites. They prophesied as a demonstration that God was working through them (Numbers 11:25). The outpouring of the Spirit on Pentecost would demonstrate in much the same way that God was working through the apostles. This was a new age. It was a new time and a new revelation. As Jesus had promised the apostles, it was not simply they who spoke, **"but the Spirit of your Father who speaks in you"** (Matthew 10:20).

The Holy Spirit's Role in Inspiration

This outpouring on the twelve was a unique thing. It did not happen to all believers. Jesus had promised the apostles, "**you shall receive power when the Holy Spirit has come upon you, and you shall be witnesses to Me in Jerusalem, and in all Judea and Samaria, and to the end of the earth**" (Acts 1:8). This miraculous power was not in all believers, yet "**through the laying on of the apostles' hands the Holy Spirit was given**" (Acts 8:18). There is no evidence in Scripture that the miraculous measure of the Holy Spirit went beyond those who received the "laying on of the apostles' hands" (see chapter five).

This brings us to the issue of the Holy Spirit's work in believers in general. If we are not careful we may confuse promises that were made to the apostles specifically with promises made to Christians generally. For example, on the night before His death Jesus' promised the twelve, "**I will pray the Father, and He will give you another Helper, that He may abide with you forever—the Spirit of truth, whom the world cannot receive, because it neither sees Him nor knows Him, but you know Him, for He dwells with you and will be in you**" (John 14:16-17). What a wonderful promise, but was it made to believers *generally* or to the apostles *specifically?* There may be some ways that the *effect* of the Holy Spirit's work would act in this way, but not everything that was true of the Spirit's work in the twelve was true of all believers. For example, we should note a number of other things Jesus told them at this same time:

> 1. He told them that the Holy Spirit "**will teach you all things, and bring to your remembrance all things that I said to you**" (John 14:16). *Who could have "remembrance" of what Jesus said?* —Only those who had been with Him in

The Holy Spirit's Role in Inspiration

the flesh. All believers have not enjoyed that privilege. The apostles were taught, **"do not worry beforehand, or premeditate what you will speak. But whatever is given you in that hour, speak that; for it is not you who speak, but the Holy Spirit"** (Mark 13:11). Yet, we notice that even Christians in the first century, such as Timothy, an evangelist (2 Timothy 4:5), who had received some miraculous spiritual gift through the laying on of hands (2 Timothy 1:6) did not have the same promise of direct teaching by the Holy Spirit. Rather, he was told to **"give attention to reading, exhortation, to doctrine"** (1 Timothy 4:13) and to **"study to shew thyself approved unto God, a workman that needeth not to be ashamed, rightly dividing the word of truth"** (2 Timothy 2:15, KJV).

2. Jesus told His apostles on the same occasion, **"The Spirit of truth, who proceeds from the Father, He will testify of Me"** (John 15:26). He did so, as Paul described with words **"which the Holy Spirit teaches, comparing spiritual things with spiritual"** (1 Corinthians 2:13). This was not a strong feeling in the heart, but understandable words revealed directly to the apostles and prophets of New Testament times (see chapter four). This *testimony* about Jesus does not come directly to all believers, as it did to the apostles.

3. Finally, He told them, **"when He, the Spirit of truth, has come, He will guide you into all truth"** (John 16:13). How much truth is "all truth"? Is there more gospel truth that has yet to be revealed to Christians? Near the end of the first century, Peter wrote, **"His divine power has given to us all**

The Holy Spirit's Role in Inspiration

> things that pertain to life and godliness" (2 Peter 1:3). Paul, in speaking of miraculous gifts such as tongues and prophecy, described them as things which were "in part" contrasting them with the time when revelation was finalized declaring, **"when that which is perfect is come, that which is in part will be done away"** (1 Corinthians 13:10). The Law of Christ contained in the New Testament revealed by the Holy Spirit is, **"the perfect law of liberty"** (James 1:25) —it is "that which is perfect."

Is there then any sense that the Holy Spirit dwells in and works in believers in general? Yes. Paul speaks of **"the sword of the Spirit, which is the word of God"** (Ephesians 6:17). It is impossible to separate the influence of someone from the word which he speaks. If I tell my children to do something, my words are the vehicle through which I *work* in them to accomplish that thing. If I write down my instructions, and they heed those instructions, the same is true. The degree to which they internalize my instructions is the degree to which they allow my *spirit* to dwell in them. The same is true of the Holy Spirit. Jesus said, **"the words that I speak to you are spirit, and they are life"** (John 6:63). The Hebrew writer said, **"the word of God is living and powerful, and sharper than any two-edged sword"** (Hebrews 4:12). It is this word, when heard that produces faith (Romans 10:17). It is by this word, revealed by the Holy Spirit, through the message of the gospel by which God's Spirit has been poured out on "all flesh" (Joel 2:28). Not all flesh receives the miraculous measure of the Holy Spirit, but in offering the message of salvation to "all flesh" it is in this way that Jesus promised that the Spirit would **"convict the world of sin"** (John 16:8).

The Holy Spirit's Role in Inspiration

God has made us spiritual beings. We are children of the "**Father of spirits**" (Hebrews 12:9). God knows our hearts and searches our spirits. Proverbs tells us, "**the spirit of man is the lamp of the Lord, searching all the inner depths of his heart**" (Proverbs 20:27). When we allow the revelation of the Holy Spirit to dwell in us it is the Spirit dwelling in us. Paul told the Ephesians that "**Christ may dwell in your hearts through faith**" (Ephesians 3:17). This is not a possession, but a choice. We are led by the Spirit when we "set our minds on" the things of the Spirit (Romans 8:5). The Christian, has the promise that God will hear their prayers always (1 John 5:15). Even, when it is difficult to know how to express the thought of the heart, as spiritual beings in contact with God's spirit, "**the Spirit Himself intercedes for us with groaning which cannot be uttered**" (Romans 8:26). What a wonderful blessing. What a glorious God! What a wonderful thought that God has revealed Himself to man and we can allow that Spirit to live in us by accepting the Spirit's revelation in the word of God—the Bible. When the Christian does that it is allowing the Spirit to work in his or her heart.

Chapter Three

The Holy Spirit's Work in the Individual Christian

The Limits of Man's Knowledge

Let us start by expressing that we must recognize the limits of our knowledge about these matters. All that we can know is what has been revealed to us. The Holy Spirit said through Moses, "**The secret things belong to the L**ORD **our God, but those things which are revealed belong to us**" (Deuteronomy 29:29). On this subject we are told that some things which God does within a Christian are "above" our capacity to think. Paul wrote that God, "**is able to do exceedingly abundantly above all that we ask or think, according to the power that works in us**" (Ephesians 3:20). Yet, the danger is that if we are not careful we may find ourselves in the same position as the false prophets of Ezekiel's day – speaking from our "own spirit." The Lord declared, "**Woe to the foolish prophets, who follow their own spirit and have seen nothing!**" (Ezekiel 13:3). If God is not the "**author of confusion**" (1 Corinthians 14:33), and

The Holy Spirit's Work in the Individual Christian

there is such a thing as the **"unity of the Spirit"** (Ephesians 4:3), we can rest assured that anything that God would do in the heart and lives of people will harmonize with what has been revealed in His word. As such, we can use Scripture to **"test all things, hold fast what is good"** (1 Thessalonians 5:21). If we find something in Scripture—we can stand on it. If we do not, we must reject it— **"Unless the Lord builds the house, they labor in vain who build it"** (Psalms 127:1).

Most people recognize that the dramatic and unquestionable events of the Holy Spirit's work in the New Testament differ from claims made today regarding miracles or direct revelation of the Spirit. In spite of this many attribute a number of questionable things to the direct operation of the Holy Spirit. The question arises, *"what, if anything, are the current functions of the Holy Spirit for or inside a believer?"* Let's try to answer this question.

What Is "Spirit"?

Part of the difficulty comes from the fact that so little has been revealed to us about exactly what "spirit" is. We are given all that we need to know, but there are undoubtedly many "secret things" on this subject which we have not been told. We know that **"God is Spirit"** (John 4:24). We know that God is said to **"fill heaven and earth"** (Jeremiah 23:24). We know that **"a spirit does not have flesh and bones"** (Luke 24:37). We know that **"there is a spirit in man, and the breath of the Lord gives him understanding"** (Job 32:8). This is said of all of mankind in general. This "spirit" within is a means by which God can know our hearts. Proverbs 20:7 teaches

The Holy Spirit's Work in the Individual Christian

us, "The spirit of man is the lamp of the LORD, searching all the inner depths of the heart." We are all children of the "**Father of spirits**" (Hebrews 12:9). As such...

> **If He should set His heart on it, if He should gather to Himself His Spirit and His breath, all flesh would perish together, And man would return to dust** (Job 34:14-15).

So, all of us only live by the mercy and continued power of God. God created laws of nature which continue to function, but it is also true that **"in Him all things consist"** (Colossians 1:17). Therefore, when He "gathers to Himself His Spirit" then, Ecclesiastes tells us **"the spirit will return to God who gave it"** (Ecclesiastes 12:7). Thus James tells us, **"the body without the spirit is dead"** (James 2:26).

"Spirit" or "spirit"?

We should note here that some translations use the custom of capitalizing what translators believe are references to Deity, as a sign of respect. In most cases the context makes it clear if the text is talking about God's "Spirit" or a created "spirit." However, sometimes this is subject to the judgment of the translator. Neither Hebrew nor New Testament Greek used such a convention. So, just because a passage may say "Spirit" instead of "spirit" doesn't necessarily mean it is a reference to Deity.

The Holy Spirit's Work in the Individual Christian

Spirit in the Sense of "Mindset" or Disposition"

Scripture will speak of "spirit" in different ways. There is "spirit" in the sense of the inner life force of a person that is made in the image of God and survives the death of the body (James 2:26). However, there is also "spirit" in the sense of one's inner mindset or disposition. Christian women are to have a **"gentle and quiet spirit"** (1 Peter 3:4). We see there can be a **"spirit of gentleness"** (1 Corinthians 4:21); a **"spirit of bondage"** (Romans 8:15); a **"spirit of faith"** (2 Corinthians 4:13) a **"spirit of stupor"** (Romans 11:8), or a **"spirit of error"** (1 John 4:6). Sometimes this mindset or disposition may come at the influence of another spirit that is evil. Paul speaks of **"the spirit who now works in the sons of disobedience"** (Ephesians 2:2). Yet, sometimes the mindset that is patterned after such an evil influence is also said to be **"the spirit of the world"** (1 Corinthians 2:12). In such an instance it is unclear if it is the mindset that is *like* the "spirit of the world" or a separate evil spirit that is being referenced. It is also unclear when this is direct (as in the case of possession) or indirect. Jesus told those who opposed Him, **"you are of your father the devil and the desires of your father you want to do"** (John 8:44). It is a mistake to imagine that every time one is said to follow the influence of evil it is due to direct influence. We are personally to blame for our own choices and our own sins. The Holy Spirit teaches us through James, **"each one is tempted when he is drawn away by his own desires and enticed"** (James 1:14).

It might seem strange to us, that both a *mindset* and the *inner life force* can both be referred to as "spirit," but if we look at how Scripture views man it is not as confusing as it might seem. Scripture teaches that we are spiritual beings interacting with other spiritual beings.

The Holy Spirit's Work in the Individual Christian

This is true whether we are talking about our interaction with God, evil spirits, or our interaction with other people. Paul warned the Corinthians, **"For if someone comes to you and preaches a Jesus other than the Jesus we preached, or if you receive a different spirit from the one you received, or a different gospel from the one you accepted, you put up with it easily enough"** (2 Corinthians 11:4-5). John taught that we must **"test the spirits, whether they are from God, for many false prophets have gone out into the world"** (1 John 4:1). How does one *test* or *receive* a "spirit"? We cannot see a spirit. The only way that we can test another person's spirit is by testing what he teaches. The faith, doctrine, disposition, and mindset of a person, reflects whether his or her spirit is in harmony with the things of God or in harmony with "the spirit of this world." Scripture describes our choice to follow a particular mindset as following a certain "spirit." This is what Paul calls **"the spirit of your mind"** (Ephesians 4:23).

"What Manner of Spirit You Are of"

We see this sense of the word "spirit" when James and John ask to call down fire on the cities that rejected Jesus. He told them, **"You do not know what manner of spirit you are of"** (Luke 9:55). In a similar situation, when Peter told Jesus that He would not be put to death, Jesus told him, **"Get behind me Satan! For you are not mindful of the things of God."** (Matthew 16:23). Certainly, Scripture describes Satan exerting direct influence on people *at times*. So, we might be tempted to say here that in both instances Jesus is indicating that an evil spirit (or Satan in the case of Peter) was directly influencing these men, but is that necessarily what it means? In the case of Peter we notice, Satan is addressed with the words "Get behind me Satan!" but Peter was rebuked, "you are not

The Holy Spirit's Work in the Individual Christian

mindful." Whatever influence Satan exerted here it was not direct enough that Peter lost any personal responsibility. To whatever degree Satan acted directly, Peter shaped his own mindset in harmony with what Satan wanted.

"Spirit and Power of Elijah"

Compare this with the prophecy given about John the Baptist. Zacharias was told, "**He will go before the Lord in the spirit and the power of Elijah**" (Luke 1:17). Was Elijah directly indwelling John? Was John to be Elijah reincarnated? Absolutely not! Was it simply God's Spirit (i.e. the Holy Spirit) in John? Notice, he is told that John would go *before the Lord,* but he would do so in the *spirit and power of Elijah.* If it is just God's Spirit why is Elijah even mentioned? The point is that just as Elijah had to be brave and resist evil to call Israel back to God, John would do the same to call the Jews to prepare for the Messiah. John taught with the same disposition and mindset as Elijah—He did so "in his spirit."

"The Same Spirit"

Paul demonstrates the same use of the concept of "spirit" in his writings. He spoke of walking in the **"same spirit"** with Titus (2 Corinthians 12:18). He told the Corinthians, in his instructions to discipline the one practicing sexual immorality, that he would be with them **"present in spirit"** (1 Corinthians 5:3). There is no indication that it meant (as described elsewhere in Scripture) that the Spirit would take him somewhere. Rather, he was of one mind with them. He was united with their purpose and actions. He says to the Colossians, in the same way, **"I am with you in spirit"** (Co-

The Holy Spirit's Work in the Individual Christian

lossians 2:5). He told the Philippians that they must **"stand fast in one spirit"** (Philippians 1:27). Clearly they were not to possess one another as an evil spirit might enter into another person's body. Instead they were to share the same mindset, disposition, purpose, faith, and conduct.

The Holy Spirit in a Christian

What about the Holy Spirit in a Christian? Paul tells us that something happens to a person when he obeys the gospel. He tells the Corinthians and Ephesians that the church collectively and the believer individually becomes the "temple" or "dwelling place" of the Holy Spirit (1 Corinthians 3:16; 6:19; Ephesians 2:22). He told the Corinthians, after referring to the "one flesh" relationship of marriage, **"he who is joined to the Lord is one spirit with Him"** (1 Corinthians 6:17). We understand that in the marriage relationship "one flesh" refers to the intimate nature of the fleshly union in marriage. There are still two people, but they are physically united. In the same way, we must recognize some things about the "one spirit" relationship between man and God. First, it does not mean that we take on the wholeness of the Spirit of God. If so, "one spirit" would mean we become God. That is blasphemous! Second, it does not mean that by being "one spirit" with the Lord, we lose control of our own spirit. Even to those with the gift of prophecy, Paul said, **"the spirits of the prophets are subject to the prophets"** (1 Corinthians 14:32). Thus we must avoid, as parameters in our understanding of the work of the Holy Spirit in the Christian, any extreme which would claim that the Christian assumes Divinity or that would forfeit personal responsibility for one's own spirit.

The Holy Spirit's Work in the Individual Christian

I. The Spirit's Role in Spiritual Rebirth

One of the first things the Bible addresses with respect to the Holy Spirit's involvement in the life of a Christian has to do with spiritual rebirth. The Bible teaches that sin separates man from God (Isaiah 59:1-2). The Bible describes this as *spiritual death.* Adam was told of the tree of the knowledge of good and evil, **"the day that you eat of it you will surely die"** (Genesis 2:17). He did not die physically when he sinned, but he was spiritually alienated from God the moment he sinned. So it is with all of Adam's descendents who follow his example. Whenever one, with the mental capacity and moral maturity to stand accountable before God first sins, he or she becomes separated from God and spiritually dead. This is what Paul told the Ephesians about their life (and his life) before coming to Christ, **"we were dead in trespasses"** (Ephesians 2:5). For this to change, Jesus taught that a person must be "born again." Jesus told Nicodemus, **"unless one is born of water and the Spirit, he cannot enter the kingdom of God"** (John 3:5).

Birth of "Water" and the "Spirit"

Jesus mentioned two things here: "water" and "Spirit." The common Protestant explanation of the first part of this argues that Jesus was referring to natural birth (cf. John 3:6). However, it was not until the time of the Reformation that this interpretation began to be used. The Scriptural evidence of a birth involving "water" which allows one entrance into the "kingdom of God" is that the Lord is speaking of baptism. Jesus commanded baptism in connection with making disciples (Matthew 28:19). Jesus connected baptism with salvation (Mark 16:16). Paul was told that baptism "washes away sins" (Acts 22:16). He then taught that in baptism one is **"baptized**

The Holy Spirit's Work in the Individual Christian

into Christ" (Romans 6:3); "**united with Christ in the likeness of His death**" (Romans 6:5); and "puts on Christ" (Galatians 3:27). Peter even went so far as to say that "**baptism now saves you**" by the resurrection of Christ as something which is "**an appeal to God for a good conscience**" (1 Peter 3:21, NASB). Protestants, in the face of a Roman Catholic environment that taught salvation by merit, falsely rejected baptism's connection with salvation altogether, concluding (mistakenly) that if it was necessary for salvation, it would make it "salvation by works." Thus, they exchanged one extreme for another extreme.

Our focus, however, is the second element of Jesus' statement—born "of the Spirit." Paul makes a parallel reference to John 3:6 in his epistle to Titus. He speaks of the, "**washing of regeneration and renewing of the Spirit**" (Titus 3:5). The blood of Jesus offers payment for sins, yet the Spirit here is said to offer "renewing." On the day of Pentecost, when Peter was asked, "**what shall we do?**" (Acts 2:37) he told the people, "**Repent, and let every one of you be baptized in the name of Jesus Christ for the remission of sins; and you shall receive the gift of the Holy Spirit**" (Acts 2:38). It is difficult in this passage to determine if the *gift* is the indwelling of the Spirit (promised elsewhere) or the gift *provided by* the Holy Spirit. Paul told the Romans, "**the wages of sin is death, but the gift of God is eternal life**" (Romans 6:23). Is there any sense in which the two are one in the same?

"The Spirit Gives Life"

Jesus taught, "**it is the Spirit that gives life**" (John 6:63). Paul used the same words, comparing Mosaic Law and the gospel, declaring, "**the letter kills, but the Spirit gives life**" (2 Corinthians 3:6). Jesus explained:

The Holy Spirit's Work in the Individual Christian

"If anyone thirsts, let him come to Me and drink. He who believes in Me, as the Scripture has said, out of his heart will flow rivers of living water." But this He spoke concerning the Spirit, whom those believing in Him would receive; for the Holy Spirit was not yet given, because Jesus was not yet glorified (John 7:37-39)

Here we note four things:
- One who thirsts must "come to" Jesus and "drink."
- One who "believes" will have "rivers of living water" flowing out of his heart.
- This promise refers to the "Holy Spirit" whom believers would "receive."
- These things could only happen after Jesus was "glorified."

Extreme Reactions

One of our first answers then, to the question of what the Holy Spirit does for the Christian, is that the "Spirit gives life." In this matter, the extremes of the religious world have often shaped our understanding of what this means. Men such as Luther and Calvin, in their rejection of the Catholicism of their day, focused on the idea of *spiritual death*. They asked the question, "how can a dead man do anything?" That was a good question. In their day there were those who actually believed that you could purchase a certificate known as an "indulgence" that claimed to grant to the purchaser forgiveness of sins, past, present, and *future!* They properly recognized how utterly unscriptural such a concept was. Yet, in their reaction to this error they went to

The Holy Spirit's Work in the Individual Christian

> another extreme. They reasoned, if a dead man can't do anything, then it must be *all the work of God.* Now certainly, when man sins, there is nothing that man can do to forgive that sin—however, there is a difference between meeting conditions for receiving God's grace and works of merit.

In this extreme reaction men like Luther and Calvin interpreted truths such as "the Spirit gives life" in an extreme manner as well. They concluded (mistakenly) that Adam's sin corrupted man to such an extent that we are "incapable of doing any good and wholly inclined towards all evil" (as one creed fashioned after their teachings claimed). If this was true what would it mean if it is "the Spirit that gives life"? In their view it was the Spirit that empowered a person to enable him to overcome the corruption of Adam's sin. What this did was eliminate personal responsibility. Both men denied that man has freewill at all. For them, it was God alone who makes us choose; God who causes man to believe; God who gives us the power to refuse sin; and even God who causes man to sin! How blasphemous! Unfortunately, most of the religious world has been influenced by these extreme views, whether they realize it or not.

How Does the "Spirit Give Life"?

Regarding the sense in which "it is the Spirit that gives life"—part of the difficulty of this issue rests in the influence human doctrines have had on our perception of Biblical teaching. We noticed above how human concepts about spiritual death influence one's interpretation of Scripture. If, as many have taught, spiritual death means

The Holy Spirit's Work in the Individual Christian

we lose all ability to obey, believe, repent, confess, and follow the instructions of God, then it would have to mean that God, through the Holy Spirit gives the one who is dead the power to do those things. If on the other hand, the Bible teaches that spiritual death is a separation from God, then yes, it is God who sets the terms of reconciliation, but it is within man to accept those terms. As such, the Holy Spirit, through the word, articulates those terms. The Holy Spirit, through the word, works in the heart to change the character and behavior of a person. Then, having been reconciled to God, it is the contact provided internally by the Holy Spirit, in an unseen manner which allows that reconciliation to exist. So long as a person allows the Holy Spirit to dwell in him, by allowing God's word to live and work within him (cf. 1 Thessalonians 2:13), he continues in that reconciled state. This is what the Bible teaches.

II. The Spirit's Direction through the Word

What does the Bible say? We notice from Jesus' words in John 7:37-39 that one who thirsts must "come to" Him. This is not compulsion, but choice. One who "believes" can enjoy this "living water" which is equated with the Holy Spirit living in him. This was available after Jesus was "glorified." This shows a Divine act of grace (Jesus' glorification on the cross paying for sin) and a Divine offer of mercy (spiritual life to one who was spiritually dead). But, we also see a human response as a condition of accepting this mercy and grace—one must "come to" Jesus and "believe." To Luther and Calvin the Spirit even made a person "come to" Jesus and "believe"—but that was not what Jesus taught. We observed earlier, that the Spirit doesn't force anything—**"the spirits of the prophets are subject to the prophets"** (1 Corinthians 14:32). In fact, Scripture does not teach that the Holy Spirit enables people *to obey* but rather it tells

The Holy Spirit's Work in the Individual Christian

us about, "**the Holy Spirit whom God has given to those who obey Him** (Acts 5:32).

Jesus' Words Are "Spirit" and "Life"

How do we understand this? Jesus' words in John 6:63 become important once again. The entire verse reads, "**It is the Spirit who gives life; the flesh profits nothing. The words that I speak to you are spirit, and they are life.**" We notice here that Jesus says His words "are spirit, and they are life." There is an inseparable relationship between what is said about the Spirit and about the message which He reveals. We see this throughout the New Testament. John tells us, "**the Spirit is the truth**" (1 John 5:6), but Jesus tells us of God, "**your word is truth**" (John 17:17). Is this a contradiction? No, it is the Spirit who reveals the word and cannot be separated from it. This is why we are told that, "**the sword of the Spirit**" is the word of God (Ephesians 6:17). As men like Calvin saw it (and many today), the word is just a "dead letter" unless the Holy Spirit acts in addition to it to give it power. That is not what Scripture teaches. The Hebrew writer said that the word is "**living and powerful**" (Hebrews 4:12). How can a message be "living"? Remember what we saw earlier, that "spirit" sometimes refers to a *mindset*. We saw in the case of John with Elijah and Titus with Paul that they were of the "same spirit." We saw in the case of Paul with Corinth or Colosse that he was "with them in spirit." If the Holy Spirit is responsible for the message of the word of God, the work of the word on the heart *is the Holy Spirit working*.

The Holy Spirit's Work in the Individual Christian

Resisting the Holy Spirit

Let us consider some examples of this in Scripture. When Paul taught the Thessalonians about practicing self-control over their bodies, he warned them, **"he who rejects this does not reject man, but God, who has also given us His Holy Spirit"** (1 Thessalonians 4:8). Stephen told the Jews, who rejected his teaching about Jesus, **"You stiffnecked and uncircumcised in heart and ears! You always resist the Holy Spirit; as your fathers did, so do you"** (Acts 7:51). How can someone *resist* the Holy Spirit? If Luther and Calvin were correct this makes no sense. The Jews who tried Stephen didn't have any personal indwelling of the Spirit. They did, however, reject the message *of the Holy Spirit*. In so doing they resisted the Holy Spirit.

"By This We Know That He Abides in Us"

Is the same thing true of believers? Let's notice John's words. He wrote, **"Now he who keeps His commandments abides in Him, and He in him. And by this we know that He abides in us, by the Spirit whom He has given us"** (1 John 3:24). Here John connects "keeping His commandments" with God abiding in a Christian. This is set parallel with "the Spirit whom He has given us" as a way to know that God "abides in us." Is this God making us follow His commandments by the compulsion of the Spirit? No. It is being "one spirit" with God by following what the Spirit has revealed. A few verses after this John says,

> No one has seen God at any time. If we love one another, God abides in us, and His love has been perfected in us. By this we know that we abide in Him, and He in us, because He has given us of His Spirit (1 John 4:12-13).

The Holy Spirit's Work in the Individual Christian

Here John says, if we love one another it allows God to be seen in us. Unbelievers love, but not in the manner, or with the motivation and purpose that the Christian does. The Christian imitates the example of Jesus. In this way God's love is "perfected" in them. This very reception of the Spirit, Paul points out to the Galatians, did not come, **"by the works of the law,"** but **"by the hearing of faith"** (Galatians 3:5). This echoes what he told the Romans, **"faith comes by hearing and hearing by the word of God"** (Romans 10:17).

Is This Salvation by Works?

Someone might ask, *isn't that salvation by works?* No! The blood of Christ saves. Man is not the one who reveals the message of salvation—that is by God's mercy. We would not know how to live on our own. When we do what we are commanded does that merit salvation? No. **"We are unprofitable servants, we have done what was our duty to do"** (Luke 17:10). Following the revealed word of the Spirit is yielding our spirit to God's. It is allowing God to work in us. It can transform our thinking. It can give us new purpose and meaning, but it is a choice not compulsion.

We have seen that the Spirit works in one who has obeyed the gospel in an unseen way to renew our spirit giving those who are spiritually dead, renewed life. We have seen that the Spirit works in us through the word to teach us and direct us. This work directly relates to two other areas in which the Spirit within becomes important: fellowship with God, and worship.

The Holy Spirit's Work in the Individual Christian

III. "The Fellowship of the Holy Spirit"

We have seen above that in sin one is spiritually separated from God, but in Christ "the spirit gives life." What does that do for our relationship with God? Second Corinthians 13:14 refers to, **"The grace of the Lord Jesus Christ, and the love of God, and the communion of the Holy Spirit."** The word translated "communion" here is the Greek word *koinonia* which is usually translated "fellowship." It is defined as, "joint participation." Philippians 2:1 echoes this, referring to, **"the fellowship of the Holy Spirit."** While Jesus is the one Mediator between God and man, having shed His blood to atone for man's sins (1 Timothy 2:5), the Bible teaches that the Holy Spirit plays a role in granting this access to God. Paul told the Ephesians, **"By Him** [i.e. by Jesus] **we both** [i.e. both the Jew and the Gentile] **have access by one Spirit** [i.e. the Holy Spirit] **to the Father"** (Ephesians 2:18). This is a very important role! Through the Spirit the Christian is granted spiritual access "to the Father." No longer must sin separate him from God. Christ's blood pays the debt—the Holy Spirit grants us fellowship to God.

IV. The Spirit in Worship

This then has an important effect on the Christian's worship. In sin, we learn, **"One who turns away his ear from hearing the law, even his prayer is an abomination"** (Proverbs 28:9). Since the blood of Christ grants one access through the Spirit, prayer is heard and worship is accepted. Jesus taught the woman at the well, **"God is Spirit, and those who worship Him must worship in spirit and truth"** (John 4:24). Notice, there is *true* worship, so by inference there can be *false* worship. How can we know what we should and should not do to worship God? When we follow the revelation of

The Holy Spirit's Work in the Individual Christian

the Spirit through the word we are worshipping "in spirit and truth." Here is where the real problem comes with some people's understanding of this issue. I have heard people try to justify things that they do in worship of God which have not been authorized by the Holy Spirit in the word by saying "the Spirit has led me to do this." That is a contradiction in terms. If it is not in the word, the Spirit cannot be *leading us*. Jude instructed us to, "**contend earnestly for the faith which was once for all delivered to the saints**" (Jude 3).

"Worship in Spirit"

When Christians follow the revelation of the Spirit, in their worship of God the access which the Spirit grants them to the Father allows them to be "one Spirit" with the Lord. It allows them to "**worship in Spirit**" (Ephesians 3:3). Christians can "**sing in the Spirit**" (1 Corinthians 14:15-16). They may "glorify God in the Spirit" (1 Corinthians 6:20). They can "pray in the Spirit" (Ephesians 6:18; Jude 20). Modern charismatic movements have led many to imagine that this is some type of ecstatic state. A careful examination of Scripture reveals that such ecstatic behavior has more to do with pagan worship than it does with New Testament worship of God in Christ. Paul wrote, "**let all things be done decently and in order**" (1 Corinthians 14:40). As we have previously observed, even when miraculous spiritual gifts were in operation, Paul taught, "**the spirits of the prophets are subject to the prophets**" (1 Corinthians 14:32). Instead of this, Paul teaches us that worship is Spirit allows those in fellowship with God in Christ, who follow the revelation of the Spirit in Scripture the assurance that they have access to God when they worship. He teaches us this about prayer specifically. He writes:

The Holy Spirit's Work in the Individual Christian

> ...The Spirit also helps in our weaknesses. For we do not know what we should pray for as we ought, but the Spirit Himself makes intercession for us with groanings which cannot be uttered. Now He who searches the hearts knows what the mind of the Spirit is, because He makes intercession for the saints according to the will of God (Romans 8:26-27).

What weakness is mentioned? The Christian doesn't always know what to pray for. Does that mean that God will remain unaware of the Christians need? No! The "Spirit Himself makes intercession." We have seen that Christ is the "one Mediator"—is this a contradiction of that doctrine? No! We are spiritual beings. God is Spirit. Being reconciled back to God, the *searching of the heart* done by the Holy Spirit allows the Father to know the needs of the heart. Is this through (as our charismatic friends say) some private prayer language? No! It takes place, "with groanings which cannot be uttered." The Christian doesn't need to call God on the phone, or send Him a letter—silently, in the heart, through the Spirit they have contact with God.

V. The "Seal" and "Guarantee" of the Holy Spirit.

This leads us to a few final questions regarding the Holy Spirit: *what is the "seal," "deposit," (or "earnest") of the Spirit?* and *what effect does the Holy Spirit have on a Christian's behavior or avoidance of sin?* Let's start with Ephesians 1:13-14:

> In Him you also trusted, after you heard the word of truth, the gospel of your salvation; in whom also, having believed, you were sealed with the Holy Spirit of promise, who is the

The Holy Spirit's Work in the Individual Christian

guarantee of our inheritance until the redemption of the purchased possession, to the praise of His glory.

We notice here what we have already seen repeatedly—belief (or as it is here "trust") comes from having "heard the word of truth." Then it tells us "having believed, you were sealed with the Holy Spirit." What does this mean? In ancient times a "seal" was a metal or carved stone ring or stamp that was pressed into wax or clay to leave the impression of the king or official who owned it. It was a mark of ownership. It was an indication of approval. All over the Near East, the clay impressions of such seals (called *bullae*) have been discovered. We might think of the figure here as the Holy Spirit making an *impression* on the heart. We notice however, that this is not separate (or in addition to) the impression caused by "having believed." Rather the two are simultaneous. As one allows this *impression* to remain on the heart, it becomes a "guarantee of our inheritance." Some have imagined that the figure here is that the impression of the Spirit's seal is such that it cannot be *worn away* (so to speak) by a rejection of that impression. Is that what the Bible teaches?

"In Our Hearts As a Guarantee"

The same figure is used twice in Second Corinthians. Paul wrote:

> He who establishes us with you in Christ and has anointed us is God, who also has sealed us and given us the Spirit in our hearts as a guarantee (2 Corinthians 1:22).

Here the Christian is said to be "anointed" and "sealed" in Christ by God—who gives "the Spirit" in the heart as a "guarantee." Later in

The Holy Spirit's Work in the Individual Christian

the book he refers to this again, after talking about the wonderful time in which mortality will be "swallowed up" in life, he writes:

> **He who has prepared us for this very thing is God, who also has given us the Spirit as a guarantee** (2 Cor. 5:5).

In none of these texts do we see the idea stated that the "seal" or the "guarantee" of the Spirit is irrevocable. It is always connected with maintaining behavior that is in harmony with the revelation of the Spirit. What then is the function of the Spirit as this "deposit" or "guarantee"?

"The Spirit Bears Witness with Our Spirit"

Paul explains it in greater detail in the book of Romans. For example, he tells them, **"the Spirit Himself bears witness with our spirit that we are children of God"** (Romans 8:16). If this *earnest* is something that empowers or directly leads a person, how is it that the Spirit "bears witness *with* our spirit"? If it is all the Spirit's doing and man bears no responsibility "our spirit" is no factor at all. On the other hand, if this is teaching that the Spirit, *searches* our spirit to determine our compliance with the revelation of the Spirit through the word, that is something different. A few verses before this passage Paul wrote:

> **... If the Spirit of Him who raised Jesus from the dead dwells in you, He who raised Christ from the dead will also give life to your mortal bodies through His Spirit who dwells in you** (Romans 8:11).

The Holy Spirit's Work in the Individual Christian

Notice what we see here. There is a condition under which God will "give life to our mortal bodies." That condition is, "if the Spirit of Him who raised Jesus from the dead dwells in you." Here is the *earnest* and *seal*—if a Christian allows the direction of the Spirit through the word to leave its impression on the heart, the Spirit's searching of the heart, bears witness to this. If the Spirit bears witness that His impression stayed upon the heart, this guarantees that the Spirit will grant eternal life to a person on the day of judgment.

VI. The Holy Spirit's Work in the Behavior of a Christian.

The final issue we must consider is the effect which the Holy Spirit has on the behavior of a Christian, and how the Holy Spirit offers assistance in avoiding sin. The issue of freewill becomes a major consideration here. Paul told the Corinthians, **"But we all, with unveiled face, beholding as in a mirror the glory of the Lord, are being transformed into the same image from glory to glory, just as by the Spirit of the Lord"** (2 Corinthians 3:18). We observed above, that any concept we frame of the Holy Spirit's work must avoid the extreme of claiming that Christians become gods, and the other extreme of claiming that personal responsibility is removed. In this text we must ask, *how is it that the Holy Spirit transforms Christians into the image of God?* If this is compulsion we must ask why do Christians still sin? Is the Spirit not doing a good enough job? If instead, this transformation is effected by our choice and submission, it becomes an issue of acceptance of the message revealed by the Holy Spirit. In that case the individual is to blame for shortcomings in his or her own life.

The Holy Spirit's Work in the Individual Christian

"By the Spirit Put to Death the Deeds of the Body"

Is there no help then offered by the Holy Spirit? Paul taught the Romans:

> **For if you live according to the flesh you will die; but if by the Spirit you put to death the deeds of the body, you will live. For as many as are led by the Spirit of God, these are sons of God** (Romans 8:13-14).

In this text we are not left to ourselves to determine what it means to be "led by the Spirit of God." Only a few verses above this Paul defined living "according to the flesh" or "according to the Spirit." Notice what he said:

> **For those who live according to the flesh set their minds on the things of the flesh, but those who live according to the Spirit, the things of the Spirit** (Romans 8:5)

Here we see that being led, or living "according to the Spirit" is accomplished by "setting our minds" on the "things of the Spirit." We are personally responsible for sin. If this is to be understood in the sense of empowerment or compulsion then it is God's fault if we sin. That is not what the Bible teaches. **"God cannot be tempted by evil, nor does He Himself tempt anyone"** (James 1:13). We can know the "things of the Spirit" by meditating and applying the word, the "sword of the Spirit" into our lives. In so doing, just as in the "Parable of the Sower," the word grows in the heart to bear fruit (Matthew 13). This is the same sentiment David expressed, **"Your word I have hidden in my heart that I might not sin against**

The Holy Spirit's Work in the Individual Christian

You!" (Psalms 119:11). This allows Christians to be "**strengthened with might through His Spirit in the inner man, that Christ may dwell in your hearts through faith**" (Ephesians 3:16-17). We note that the manner in which this indwelling of Christ is described is "through faith." When Christians allow faith—which comes from hearing the word of God revealed by the Spirit—to dwell in them, it is Christ *dwelling* in them.

The Spirit's Transformation into the Image of God

The same principle is true of other ways in which the Holy Spirit is said to "transform" the Christian into the image of God. We note this in some things having to do with the tongue. Paul and John both teach us some important points on this. They both teach that no one can confess Jesus coming in the flesh, or that "Jesus is Lord" except by the Spirit of God (1 Corinthians 12:3; 1 John 4:2-3). It is clear that an unbeliever can say the words. This cannot mean that the Spirit produces the words, produces the faith, or empowers one to confess. Rather, what it is teaching is that accepting the conviction of the heart that leads one to genuinely confess Jesus is from the Holy Spirit. If this is compulsion—Calvin was right, it is not a choice nor could it be resisted. If it is acceptance of the "mindset" of the Spirit it is not God's fault if an unbeliever chooses not to confess. As a result, we can see it as a work of the Holy Spirit, when a person accepts the message of the gospel and allows that to move his heart to confession of Christ.

The Holy Spirit's Work in the Individual Christian

"Fruit of the Spirit"

We see this same principle in other types of behavior. This influence of the Holy Spirit, through acceptance and application of the word is said to lead to "joy" of the Holy Spirit (1 Thessalonians 1:6); **"love in the Spirit"** (Colossians 1:8; cf. Romans 15:30); "comfort" of the Holy Spirit (Acts 9:31); "righteousness" and "peace" (Romans 14:17) and all the other qualities described as **"fruit of the Spirit"** (Galatians 5:22; Ephesians 5:9). The Christian who follows the conduct taught in the word of God, brings forth this kind of behavior. It is the work of the Holy Spirit, accomplished through the medium of the word of God applied to the human heart.

"If We Live in the Spirit, Let Us Also Walk in the Spirit"

There is clearly an aspect of the work of the Holy Spirit which is God's part, but there is also a part which is dependent upon man's choice. When one is obedient to the gospel, the restoration of man unto God involves the Holy Spirit. Paul calls this **"living in the Spirit"** (Galatians 5:25). Yet, Paul also shows that there is an aspect of yielding to the Spirit which is man's choice. One must "walk in Spirit" (Galatians 5:16). Paul teaches, **"If we live in the Spirit, let us also walk in the Spirit"** (Galatians 5:25). In this sense one is to "be filled with the Holy Spirit" – a command (Ephesians 5:18). We must sow to the Spirit in order to reap of the Spirit eternal life (Galatians 6:8). This is our choice and it is our responsibility. If we, after coming to Christ, reject the teaching of the Holy Spirit and live "according to the flesh" Paul tells us that we **"grieve the Holy Spirit"** (Ephesians 4:30). This very fact shows that the work of the Holy Spirit is not compelled upon a person, nor wholly the work of

The Holy Spirit's Work in the Individual Christian

God, or else the Holy Spirit would be *grieving* Himself. Rather, the degree to which the Spirit dwells in a Christian is such that man's own choice can accept or reject His influence.

Summary

What have we seen so far? The Bible teaches that the Holy Spirit does the following for the individual Christian:

- "**The Spirit Gives Life**" (John 6:63).
- "**Access by One Spirit to the Father**" (Ephesians 2:18).
- "**The Spirit Himself Makes Intercession for Us**" (Romans 8:26).
- "**The Spirit Himself Bears Witness with Our Spirit**" (Romans 8:16).
- "**By the Spirit Put to Death the Deeds of the Body**" (Romans 8:13).

The first four of these items are internal, unseen, and unfelt. The last of these items operates through the "**sword of the Spirit**" (Ephesians 6:17)—"**the word of God which also effectually works**" (1 Thessalonians 2:13) in the heart of the believer to transform a person's life and behavior.

Chapter Four

When the Holy Spirit Speaks: Strong Feeling or Words?

In discussions with friends in the religious world, it is not uncommon to hear people claim that the Holy Spirit has led them to do or to say something. Such people believe strongly that the Holy Spirit leads them in a direct manner, separate from the guidance found in the word. When questioned, in most cases, what they really mean by this is that they have felt a strong feeling within which led them to say or do something. It is always important to test all things by the standard of Scripture. On this issue, this is especially important, lest we find ourselves in the same position as the false prophets in the days of Ezekiel, **"who follow their own spirit and have seen nothing"** (Ezekiel 13:3).

Are there times in Scripture when the Holy Spirit spoke to Christians through a strong feeling? As a test case we can survey the accounts in the New Testament in which we are told that the Holy Spirit spoke. As a record of the early church, and a history of the Holy Spirit's work in the church, how does it describe the Spirit's guidance to Christians?

When the Holy Spirit Speaks: Strong Feeling or Words?

There are six instances in which such direct guidance is recorded. The first example relates to the preaching of Philip to the Ethiopian nobleman. When he saw the man in his chariot, Scripture tells us: **"Then the Spirit said to Philip, 'Go near and overtake this chariot.'"** (Acts 8:29). We notice that the Spirit's communication to Philip was clear, concrete, and in the form of a complete sentence. A second example, occurred when Peter saw the vision of the sheet lowered from heaven with animals in it. Scripture records: **"While Peter thought about the vision, the Spirit said to him, 'Behold, three men are seeking you. Arise therefore, go down and go with them, doubting nothing; for I have sent them'"** (Acts 10:19-20). Here we see two complete sentences. One sentence expresses knowledge of things beyond Peter's senses (i.e. that there were three men). The second sentence commands certain behavior. These were not just vague feelings.

Two examples concern the prophet Agabus. The first reveals: **"And in these days prophets came from Jerusalem to Antioch. Then one of them, named Agabus, stood up and showed by the Spirit that there was going to be a great famine throughout all the world, which also happened in the days of Claudius Caesar"** (Acts 11:27-29). While this account does not reveal the specific words of the Spirit, the nature of the revelation indicates a great level of specificity. We note that the Spirit revealed to him there would be 1) "a famine"; 2) it would be "great"; and 3) it would span "throughout all the world." The second came when Paul was returning to Jerusalem. The text records:

> And as we stayed many days, a certain prophet named Agabus came down from Judea. When he had come to us, he took Paul's belt, bound his own hands and feet,

When the Holy Spirit Speaks: Strong Feeling or Words?

and said, Thus says the Holy Spirit, 'So shall the Jews at Jerusalem bind the man who owns this belt, and deliver him into the hands of the Gentiles'" (Acts 21:10-12).

In this revelation there is not only a complete sentence but the command from the Spirit to the prophet to use a prop—Paul's belt, to illustrate what would happen to him. We see this is much more than a strong motivation within the heart of Agabus. It is clear communication in words.

Two final examples both concern Paul. While in Antioch, we learn about prophets in the church in that city. Of these prophets, Scripture records: **"As they ministered to the Lord and fasted, the Holy Spirit said, 'Now separate to Me Barnabas and Saul for the work to which I have called them'"** (Acts 13:2-3). Here the Spirit identified men by name—"Barnabas and Saul." Here the Holy Spirit commands their appointment for a specific work. These are words which were spoken, recorded, and understandable. A final example, echoes what would be declared by Agabus. Paul relates: **"And see, now I go bound in the spirit to Jerusalem, not knowing the things that will happen to me there, except that the Holy Spirit testifies in every city, saying that chains and tribulations await me"** (Acts 20:22-23). Here, once again, the Spirit uses clear words declaring that "chains" and "tribulations" awaited Paul. This was clearly not strong feeling, it was communication which could be recorded, written down, and clearly understood.

> There is no question that the apostles were promised that the Holy Spirit would speak through them (Mark 13:11). There is also no question that the apostles were

When the Holy Spirit Speaks: Strong Feeling or Words?

promised that the Holy Spirit would directly guide them (John 16:13). These promises were not to all believers—the means through which the Holy Spirit guides believers in general is through the word of God, the **"sword of the Spirit"** (Ephesians 6:17). The pattern of Scripture is that when the Holy Spirit did speak directly to believers it was in words, **"which the Holy Spirit speaks"** (1 Corinthians 2:13). Any strong inclination of the heart which does not follow this pattern can not reliably be viewed as the guidance of the Holy Spirit.

Chapter Five

Can It Be Proven from Scripture that Miraculous Spiritual Gifts Have Ceased?

To answer this final question we offer seven points for consideration: 1) **The Definition of "Miraculous Spiritual Gifts"**; 2) **The Biblical Doctrine of "the Laying on of the Apostles' Hands"**; 3) **The Stated Purpose of Miraculous Spiritual Gifts**; 4) **Peripheral Evidence** (i.e. some things evident from the structure, preservation, and existence of Scripture); 5) **Prophetic Evidence** (i.e. evidence from Old Testament prophecy); 6) **Evidence from First Corinthians**; and finally 7) Evidence from what is taught regarding the **Binding of Satan**.

I. The Definition of "Miraculous Spiritual Gifts"

To understand the role and duration of miraculous spiritual gifts we must first understand what the Scripture teaches regarding these gifts. In general terms, these gifts are of a character which operates beyond and outside of the natural operation of the body and mind.

Does Scripture Teach Miraculous Spiritual Gifts Have Ceased?

These are distinct from gifts given by God which are non-miraculous in nature, and are distinct from promises God has made regarding the general benefits of prayer to the Christian.

A list which the Holy Spirit offers of some such gifts is found in First Corinthians 12:4-11. Let's consider each of the gifts mentioned:

"Word of Wisdom" – "Word of Knowledge" – "Faith"

(12:8-9). These gifts refer to revealed wisdom, knowledge, or elements of **"the faith which was once for all delivered to the saints"** (Jude 3). Personal faith is not *bestowed* upon a person. Rather, it comes from hearing the word of God (Romans 10:17). It is possible that the gift of "faith" might refer to *strong faith* in the same sense that Paul speaks of his own self-control as a "gift" (cf. 1 Corinthians 7:7). However, the context makes it more likely that he is talking about the revelation of information, categorized as *wisdom, knowledge* and *faith*.

"Healings" – "Working of Miracles"

(12:9-10). This is the ability to Divinely perform a miracle of healing. This is to be distinguished from simply the **"prayer of faith"** (James 5:15). While the gifts of "healings" or "working miracles" might involve prayer, this gift allowed an individual to call the power of God toward the immediate healing of another.

"Prophecy"

(12:10) is the direct revelation of information received independent of the personal study of the prophet. This was not exclusively predictive in nature. Some prophecy was simply instructive. It was not ecstatic (cf. 1 Corinthians 14:32). The prophet was in control of his or her mind and spirit.

"**Discerning of Spirits**" (12:10) is the miraculous ability to know the motive or content of the spirit within another whether human (see Acts 13:9-11) or demonic (1 Corinthians 10:20).

"**Different Kinds of Tongues**" – "**Interpretation of Tongues**" (12:10). As the account on Pentecost shows, these were human tongues. This gift allowed the bearer to communicate with other human beings in languages they had not studied. On Pentecost this involved both the ability to speak different tongues (Acts 2:4) and to be understood in one's own language (Acts 2:8). "Interpretation of tongues" would have allowed the bearer to understand another person's language in discourse (cf. 1 Corinthians 14:28). Paul's instructions to Corinth may have been given in an attempt to train them in principles by which they could distinguish genuine tongues from the ecstatic utterances they might have practiced as pagans (1 Corinthians 12:2-3).

These are not the only "gifts." Romans 12:6-8 list other gifts some of which are miraculous in nature and others which are not. Nor are these the only *works* in the church. Ephesians 4:11 lists some types of works which were dependent upon miraculous gifts and some which were not. In broad terms, miraculous spiritual gifts were gifts which enabled the bearer to use Divine power to act in ways that suspended (or overcame) laws of nature. These gifts operated under the control of the bearer of these gifts.

II. The Biblical Doctrine of "The Laying On of the Apostles' Hands"

There is a clear connection between the distribution of these gifts and the work of the apostles. The apostles held a special role in

Does Scripture Teach Miraculous Spiritual Gifts Have Ceased?

the establishment of the church. Not all disciples were apostles. We see this from the qualifications of apostles outlined in Acts 2:21-22. The apostles were not limited to the possession of simply one gift. They could prophesy, heal, perform miracles, and speak in tongues. They were, however, able to distribute gifts. This can be seen from the account of Simon who sinned in trying to buy the ability to "lay hands on" others in order to distribute gifts himself. While the text describes this as simply the "Holy Spirit" being given, the context makes it clear that this involved special gifts which were not simply given when a person obeyed the gospel. Those in Samaria obeyed the gospel, but they had not yet received the Spirit (Acts 8:17). The converts in Ephesus did not "receive the Holy Spirit" upon their baptism, but after Paul laid hands upon them. It was only then that they spoke in tongues and prophesied (Acts 19:5-6). Timothy received a gift by the laying on of Paul's hands (2 Timothy 1:6). This same instance is referred to in 1 Timothy 4:14 as the laying on of the hands of the "presbytery" (a term meaning *eldership*)—used here of the apostles as those *elder* in the faith. The church in Rome, most likely established by converts from Pentecost who returned back to Rome, had not received miraculous spiritual gifts upon the writing of Paul's epistle to them (see Romans 1:11-12). This had not yet happened because neither he (nor apparently other apostles) had yet been to Rome (see Romans 15:23). This special function of the apostles, by which miraculous spiritual gifts were distributed, is undoubtedly one of the reasons Paul told the Ephesians that the church is built upon the **"foundation of the apostles and prophets with Jesus Christ Himself as the chief cornerstone"** (Ephesians 2:20).

This special role of the apostles was unique. They did not establish a chain of *apostolic succession* (as our Roman Catholic friends try to affirm). There is no Scriptural evidence that their authority

Does Scripture Teach Miraculous Spiritual Gifts Have Ceased?

as **"ambassadors of Christ"** (2 Corinthians 5:20) passed to others beyond their death. In the same way, the special ability bestowed upon them to lay hands upon others and distribute spiritual gifts, was not passed on to others upon their death. There is no Scriptural evidence that one who received a miraculous spiritual gift had the ability to "lay hands on" others in order to distribute such gifts. As a result, upon the death of the apostles the Scriptural means to distribute spiritual gifts came to an end. Upon the death of those who had received the "laying of the hands of the apostles" all miraculous spiritual gifts came to an end.

III. The Stated Purpose of Miraculous Spiritual Gifts

Scripture reveals to us a great deal about the purpose and significance of these miraculous spiritual gifts. This helps us understand a number of things about their duration and the role which they played in the establishment of the Lord's church. In Mark's account of the Great Commission Jesus promised:

> **And these signs will follow those who believe: In My name they will cast out demons; they will speak with new tongues; they will take up serpents; and if they drink anything deadly, it will by no means hurt them; they will lay hands on the sick, and they will recover** (Mark 16:17-18).

There is no question that these signs truly did "follow those who believed." Yet, the Holy Spirit, goes further to tell us about this, declaring:

Does Scripture Teach Miraculous Spiritual Gifts Have Ceased?

> So then, after the Lord had spoken to them, He was received up into heaven, and sat down at the right hand of God. And they went out and preached everywhere, the Lord working with them and confirming the word through the accompanying signs. Amen (Mark 16:19-20).

Here the Holy Spirit declares a purpose for these gifts. Through these gifts the Lord demonstrated that He was "working with them" in order to "confirm" the word "through the accompanying signs. Was this confirmation personal in nature? In other words, did the Lord provide a miracle or sign to every individual in doubt in order to confirm the validity of the message? No. In Acts 17:32, after preaching to those in Athens, no miracle is offered in spite of the fact that **"some mocked"** while others asked to hear Paul again. It is also clear that these gifts were not intended to grant deliverance and healing to all who were sick. Paul states plainly that he left a companion named Trophimus sick in Miletus (2 Timothy 4:20). Paul certainly could have healed him, but it was not done. It is evident that these miraculous gifts were intended to collectively demonstrate the Divine nature of the message of salvation that was being preached in Jesus Christ. The Hebrew writer declares the same fact, speaking of the "great salvation" taught in Christ:

> ... Which at the first began to be spoken by the Lord, and was confirmed to us by those who heard Him, God also bearing witness both with signs and wonders, with various miracles, and gifts of the Holy Spirit, according to His own will (Hebrews 2:3-4).

Here the Hebrew writer states in essence what Mark declared. In these *signs, wonders,* and *various miracles* God showed Himself to be

Does Scripture Teach Miraculous Spiritual Gifts Have Ceased?

"bearing witness" as a means of confirmation of the message. With this as a stated purpose of these miraculous spiritual gifts, we must consider *does God need to continue to bear witness to a word that has been confirmed?* Many in modern times seem to feel as if the New Testament "witness" of God is insufficient. It must be understood that these gifts, which served both to reveal the word and then confirm its validity were never intended to serve as a constant and ongoing process of revelation and confirmation. The Holy Spirit Himself tells us that they offered confirmation. A message that has been confirmed to be Divine, needs no further "witness" to establish its validity.

IV. Peripheral Evidence

There can be no dispute that there have been times in history when God has been silent in regard to the revelation of Scripture.

- From creation until the giving of the Law of Moses, there is no Scriptural evidence of any revealed Scripture. God did, however, speak to some Patriarchs directly.
- Between the Old and New Testaments there was a 400 year period in which there was no Scripture revealed. The examples of Simeon (Luke 2:25-26) and Anna (Luke 2:36-38) show that there may have been some prophetic revelation during this period, in spite of the fact that there was no Scripture revealed.
- Since the writing of the book of Revelation, there has been no Scripture revealed.

Does Scripture Teach Miraculous Spiritual Gifts Have Ceased?

At the very least this proves that the miraculous spiritual gift which led to the inspiration of Scripture has ceased.

V. Prophetic Evidence

Two Old Testament passages address matters related to the issue of miraculous spiritual gifts: Joel 2:28-29 and Zechariah 13:1-6.

- Joel 2:28-29 promised:
  And it shall come to pass afterward that I will pour out My Spirit on all flesh; your sons and your daughters shall prophesy, your old men shall dream dreams, your young men shall see visions. And also on My menservants and on My maidservants I will pour out My Spirit in those days.

Peter identifies the time of the commencement of this on the Day of Pentecost after Jesus' ascension (Acts 2:16). While Joel mentions only *prophecy, dreams, and visions* the inference of the "pouring out of the Spirit" in light of New Testament suggests that this involved other gifts as well, such as tongues, healings, etc. Yet, this is not the only Old Testament reference to miraculous spiritual gifts in the age of Christ.

- Zechariah 13:1-6 promised:
  "**In that day a fountain shall be opened for the house of David and for the inhabitants of Jerusalem, for sin and for uncleanness. It shall be in that day,**" says the LORD of hosts, "**that I will cut off the names of the idols from the land, and they shall no longer be remembered. I will also cause the prophets and the unclean spirit to depart**

Does Scripture Teach Miraculous Spiritual Gifts Have Ceased?

> from the land. It shall come to pass that if anyone still prophesies, then his father and mother who begot him will say to him, 'You shall not live, because you have spoken lies in the name of the LORD.' And his father and mother who begot him shall thrust him through when he prophesies. And it shall be in that day that every prophet will be ashamed of his vision when he prophesies; they will not wear a robe of coarse hair to deceive. But he will say, 'I am no prophet, I am a farmer; for a man taught me to keep cattle from my youth.' "And one will say to him, 'What are these wounds between your arms?' Then he will answer, 'Those with which I was wounded in the house of my friends.'"

The time of this prophecy's fulfillment is identified as when a "fountain" is opened for David's house and Jerusalem, "for sin and uncleanness." The only *fountain* that has flowed from Jerusalem for "sin" is the "living water" (cf. Zechariah 14:8 & John 4:10-11) that has flowed forth through the Gospel, which was first preached from Jerusalem. While much of this passage does focus on the "cutting off" of the false prophet—it nonetheless speaks of a time when "the prophets" and the "unclean spirit" will depart from the land. While the New Testament does not explicitly identify when this prophecy was fulfilled 1 Corinthians 13:10 may indicate when this time would be. [Note: We shall return to 1 Corinthians 13:10 below].

At the very least the prophetic evidence shows that during the period of the New Covenant there will be not only a period of the outpouring of miraculous spiritual gifts but also a time in which *at least the gift of prophecy* will cease. The fact that Joel uses *prophecy, dreams, and visions* to refer to all miraculous spiritual gifts, may

Does Scripture Teach Miraculous Spiritual Gifts Have Ceased?

infer that Zechariah uses reference to the *prophet* and *evil spirit* in the same way in reference to miraculous spiritual gifts collectively.

VI. Evidence from First Corinthians

The apostle Paul devotes three chapters in his first letter to the Corinthians to the issue of spiritual gifts. He begins in 12:1 with the words, **"Now concerning spiritual gifts brethren, I do not want you to be ignorant."** He then proceeds to address issues primarily relating to tongues and prophecy in the assembly summarizing in 14:40: **"Let all things be done decently and in order."** In the midst of this he offers the beautiful chapter which teaches us the true nature of love, in 13:1-8a. After this he declares the following:

> …But whether there are prophecies, they will fail; whether there are tongues, they will cease; whether there is knowledge, it will vanish away. For we know in part and we prophesy in part. But when that which is perfect has come, then that which is in part will be done away (1 Corinthians 13:8-10).

Here the Holy Spirit declares plainly through the mouth of Paul that there will be a time in which "prophecies will fail," "tongues will cease," and "knowledge will vanish away." The time when this will occur is identified. These gifts mentioned, of *prophecy, tongues* and (by inference) *revealed knowledge,* are described as things that were only "in part." This is an important declaration. In spite of the views of modern charismatics these gifts were never to represent the *fullness* of God's interaction with man. They were not an end unto themselves, but were something "in part." Paul told us these things would end, "when that which is perfect has come." There are four ways this is usually explained:

Does Scripture Teach Miraculous Spiritual Gifts Have Ceased?

1. The return of Christ. If this idea was correct it would be reasonable to expect the text to say—"when He who is perfect has come." In the Greek the word translated "perfect" is a neuter adjective. This is why it is translated "that which," rather than "He who."

2. The state of the saved in heaven. Many lean toward this view largely due to verse twelve—"**Then I shall know just as I also am known.**" The problem with this is the declaration of verse 8 that knowledge will "vanish away." In what sense will knowledge vanish away in heaven? If it is common knowledge surely it isn't suggesting that we will lose our ability to reason. If it is miraculous knowledge, won't heaven be the ultimate revelation of the mind of God? [Note: We'll go back to verse twelve again below.]

3. A mature church. This idea would harmonize well with Ephesians 4:11-16 which speaks of different gifts being given – "**till we all come to the unity of the faith and the knowledge of the Son of God, to a perfect man, to the measure of the stature of the fullness of Christ**" (v. 13). However, one would have to concede that such occurred in the first century. Jude spoke of the faith—"**Which was once for all delivered to the saints**" (v. 3) and Peter claims of God that—"**His divine power has given to us all things that pertain to life and godliness**" (2 Peter 1:3). Further, the context of First Corinthians thirteen doesn't concern the incomplete (or immature) nature of the church, but rather the incomplete nature of revelation. All of this leads us to favor a fourth explanation...

Does Scripture Teach Miraculous Spiritual Gifts Have Ceased?

> **4. Complete revelation.** The Greek word translated "perfect" is the word *telion* meaning—"brought to its end, finished; wanting nothing necessary to completeness; perfect" (Thayer, 618). The context of Paul's teaching concerns partial revelation. The early church had been given miraculous spiritual gifts to confirm their message (Mark 16:20) and to complete God's revelation to man (John 16:13 & 14:26). This partial nature of God's revelation was fully accomplished by the time late New Testament writers composed their works (Jude 3 & 2 Peter 1:3). This revelation is preserved for us in the form of the written words of New Testament Scripture. It is this message which James calls the **"perfect law of liberty"** (James 1:25). Thus it is reasonable, Scriptural, and contextual to conclude that, "that which is perfect" is the full and complete revelation of New Testament Scripture, which has now come. This tells us, as a result, that, "that which is in part" (i.e. miraculous spiritual gifts) are "done away."

We should note an interesting element in Paul's words in 1 Corinthians 13:12. The text reads:

> **For now we see in a mirror, dimly, but then face to face. Now I know in part, but then I shall know just as I also am known.**

If we had this verse alone with no other context of Paul's meaning here, we might conclude that heaven will be the only time in which the Christian will behold the Lord "face to face." However, there is a very significant history behind this phrase. Five times in the Law

Does Scripture Teach Miraculous Spiritual Gifts Have Ceased?

of Moses, it is used of the relationship between God, Moses and Israel. Exodus 33:11 says, **"the Lord spoke to Moses face to face."** In Numbers 12:8 God says of Moses, **"I will speak with him face to face."** Then in Numbers 14:14, the Holy Spirit tells us, **"You, Lord, are among these people; ... You, Lord, are seen face to face."** In the same way Moses told the people, **"The Lord talked with you face to face on the mountain from the midst of the fire"** (Deuteronomy 5:4). And finally, Deuteronomy ends, saying of Moses, **"But since then there has not arisen in Israel a prophet like Moses, whom the Lord knew face to face"** (Deuteronomy 34:10). It is evident that none of these statements suggests that Moses (or Israel collectively) saw the full glory of the *face* of God. John tells us, **"no one has seen God at any time"** (John 1:18; 1 John 4:12). Nor is it saying that Moses and Israel were in the presence of God in heaven. Rather, it is describing a fullness, and complete measure of revelation which was unequalled at the time. God in giving the Law of Moses, of which the Psalmist said, **"the Law of the Lord is perfect, converting the soul"** (Psalms 19:7), established a relationship with Israel which was described as one that was "face to face." Paul uses the same figure speaking of the time in which the New Covenant would be fully revealed as a time when "that which is perfect" would come—a time in which Christians, in their relationship with God (just like Moses and Israel) would see the will of God "face to face."

VII. The Binding of Satan

One final factor which enters into this issue concerns the teaching of Revelation 20:1-4 regarding the binding of Satan. The text reads:

> Then I saw an angel coming down from heaven, having the key to the bottomless pit and a great chain in his hand. He laid hold of the dragon, that serpent of old, who is the Devil and Satan, and bound him for a thousand years; and he cast him into the bottomless pit, and shut him up, and set a seal on him, so that he should deceive the nations no more till the thousand years were finished. But after these things he must be released for a little while. And I saw thrones, and they sat on them, and judgment was committed to them. Then I saw the souls of those who had been beheaded for their witness to Jesus and for the word of God, who had not worshiped the beast or his image, and had not received his mark on their foreheads or on their hands. And they lived and reigned with Christ for a thousand years.

This texts speaks of a time in which "Satan" is *bound* for a period of "one thousand years." This period is identified as taking place when Christ "reigns." The evidence of the New Testament is that the kingdom and reign of Christ began with His resurrection from the dead, conquering death. Prior to His ascension Jesus declared Himself to have **"all authority"** over a realm He says is **"in heaven and on earth"** (Matthew 28:18). Christians in the first century already considered themselves to be a part of His kingdom. Paul told the Colossians, **"He has delivered us from the power of dark-**

Does Scripture Teach Miraculous Spiritual Gifts Have Ceased?

ness and conveyed us into the kingdom of the Son of His love" (Colossians 1:13). John, in the Book of Revelation itself, identified himself saying, "**I John, both your brother and companion in the tribulation and kingdom and patience of Jesus Christ**" (Revelation 1:9). This makes it clear that Christ has *reigned* from the time of His ascension to the present. As such, the period of "one thousand years" must be understood to be a large period of time—but not a literal "one thousand years." This being the case, it indicates that during the time of Christ's reign over His kingdom, the church, Satan is *bound*. In light of Zechariah 13:1-6 this appears to refer to a period of restricted demonic activity during the time of Christ's reign. If this is correct, and the "evil spirit" is caused to pass from the land, the need for the power to "cast out evil spirits" would itself be eliminated. It is unclear what Revelation 20:3 indicates about the period in which Satan shall be "released for a little while." If is does indicate a period of renewed demonic activity, there is no doubt that Christians would be given whatever would be needed to overcome any such influence.

Conclusion

In light of this evidence I believe that it is proven from Scripture that the miraculous spiritual gifts bestowed upon the New Testament church came to an end when the means of distributing those gifts through the "laying on of the apostles' hands" died with the apostles. It is clear from Scripture that these gifts were not intended to be permanent. Not all Christians were healed or could heal. It is clear that these gifts were only to endure until the coming of "that which is perfect." In the light of the context, miraculous spiritual gifts (which were "in part") are contrasted with "that which is perfect (i.e. complete revelation). These gifts were not intended to

Does Scripture Teach Miraculous Spiritual Gifts Have Ceased?

confirm personal belief—many who might have believed were left to their own unbelief. They were however, to serve collectively as Divine confirmation of the validity of the message of the gospel. With the completion of the New Testament, the need for additional revelation of the gospel came to an end. With the validity of the gospel established, the need for such confirmation came to an end. Divine silence regarding additional revelation of Scripture since the completion of the New Testament provides further evidence that the special work of the Holy Spirit in miraculous spiritual gifts given to the New Testament church has ceased.

Scripture Index

Genesis
2:17 23
Exodus
33:11 57
Numbers
11:25 11
12:8 57
14:14 57
Deuteronomy
5:4 57
29:29 .... 9, 16
34:10 57
Job
32:8 17
34:14-15 18
Psalms
19:7 57
119:11 38
127:1 17
Proverbs
20:27 15
28:9 31
Ecclesiastes
12:7 18
Isaiah
59:1-2 23
Jeremiah
23:24 17

Ezekiel
13:3 1 .... 6, 41
Joel
2:28 14
2:28-29 .... 11, 52
Zechariah
13:1-6 .... 53, 59
13:1-6. 52
14:8 53
Matthew
10:20 .... 8, 11
13 37
16:23 20
22:43 10
28:18 58
28:19 .... 7, 23
Mark
13:11 .... 13, 43
16:16 23
16:17-18 49
16:19-20 50
16:20 56
Luke
1:17 21
3:21-22 9
9:55 20
17:10 30
2:25-26 52
2:36-38 52
22:42 .... 7, 8

61

Scripture Index

24:37 17
John
1:18 57
3:5 23
3:6 .... 23, 24
4:10-11 53
4:24 .... 17, 32
6:63 .... 14, 24, 28, 40
7:37-39 .... 25, 27
8:44 19
14:16 12
14:16-17 12
14:26 56
15:26 13
16:13 .... 7, 8, 13, 44, 56
16:8 14
17:17 28

Acts
1:8 12
2:16 .... 11, 52
2:21-22 48
2:37 24
2:38 24
2:4 47
2:8 47
5:32 28
7:51 29
8:17 48
8:18 12
8:29 42
9:31 39
10:19-20 42
11:27-29 42
13:2-3 43
13:9-11 47
17:32 50
19:5-6 48
20:22-23 43

21:10-12 43
22:16 23
Romans
1:11-12 48
6:3 24
6:5 24
6:23 24
8:5 .... 15, 37
8:11 35
8:13 40
8:13-14 37
8:15 19
8:16 .... 35, 40
8:26 .... 15, 40
8:26-27 33
10:17 .... 14, 30, 46
11:8 19
12:6-8 47
14:17 39
15:23 48
15:30 39

1 Corinthians
2:12 19
2:13 .... 13, 44
3:16 22
4:21 19
5:3 21
6:17 22
6:19 .... 8, 22
6:20 32
7:7 46
8:6 7
10:20 47
12:1 54
12:10 .... 46, 47
12:2-3 47
12:3 38
12:4-11 46

Scripture Index

12:8-9	46
12:9-10	46
13:1-8a	54
13:10	14, 53, 54
13:12	57
13:8-10	54
14:15-16	32
14:28	47
14:32	22, 27, 32, 46
14:33	16
14:40	32, 54

2 Corinthians

1:22	34
3:18	36
3:6	24
4:13	19
5:20	49
5:5	35
11:4-5	20
12:18	21
13:14	31

Galatians

3:27	24
3:5	30
4:6	8
5:16	39
5:22	39
5:25	39
6:8	39

Ephesians

1:13-14	33
2:18	31, 40
2:2	19
2:20	48
2:22	22
2:5	23
3:16-17	38
3:17	15
3:20	16
3:3	32
4:11	47
4:11-16	55
4:23	20
4:3	17
4:30	39
5:18	39
5:9	39
6:17	14, 28, 40, 44
6:18	32

Philippians

1:27	22
2:1	31

Colossians

1:13	59
1:17	18
1:8	39
2:5	21

1 Thessalonians

1:6	39
2:13	27, 40
4:8	29
5:21	17

1 Timothy

2:5	31
4:13	13
4:14	48

2 Timothy

1:6	13, 48
2:15	13
3:16	10
4:20	50
4:5	13

Titus

3:5	24

Scripture Index

Hebrews
- 12:9 .... 15, 18
- 2:3-4 51
- 4:12 .... 14, 28

James
- 1:13 37
- 1:14 19
- 1:25 .... 14, 56
- 2:26 .... 18, 19
- 5:15 46

1 Peter
- 3:21 24
- 3:4 19

2 Peter
- 1:20,21 10
- 1:3 14, ... 56

1 John
- 3:24 29
- 4:1 20
- 4:12 57
- 4:12-13 29
- 4:2-3 38
- 4:6 19
- 5:15 15
- 5:6 28

Jude
- 3 .... 32, 46, 56
- 20 32

Revelation
- 1:9 59
- 20:1-4 58
- 20:3 59

www.ingramcontent.com/pod-product-compliance
Lightning Source LLC
Chambersburg PA
CBHW061343040426
42444CB00011B/3057